A Simple Schedule C Expense Tracker for Sole Proprietors, Single-Member LLCs, Freelancers, and Independent Contractors

AF873746

By Amy Rose Herrick, ChFC

By Amy Rose Herrick, ChFC

A Simple Schedule C Expense Tracker for Sole Proprietors, Single-Member LLCs, Freelancers, and Independent Contractors

First edition
Christiansted, US Virgin Islands: Amy Rose Herrick, 2026

v, 115 pages, 8.5 by 11 inches

Business | Accounting Records and Bookkeeping | Sole Proprietors | Schedule C Filers

ISBN 978-1-960427-56-4

Library of Congress Control Number: Not assigned

657.93

This Book Belongs To

Name: ______________________________

Business Name: ______________________________

Tax Year: ______________________________

Contact Info: ______________________________

____

Table of Contents

Introduction

Good recordkeeping is one of the most overlooked and most valuable habits of running a successful business.

This workbook was created to make tracking Schedule C expenses, supporting worksheets, and year-end totals easier, more accurate, and far less stressful.

Rather than scrambling at tax time or trying to reconstruct expenses months later, this resource is designed to be used consistently throughout the year.

Each section mirrors common IRS reporting categories and separates complex areas such as home office, self-employed health insurance, mileage, depreciation, and cost of goods sold so they can be tracked clearly and reviewed accurately.

This book is not a substitute for professional tax advice.

Instead, it is a practical organizational tool meant to work **alongside** your tax professional, software, or payroll system.

When used properly, it helps reduce errors, improve compliance, and save time by keeping everything in one place.

Whether you prepare your own return or work with a professional, accurate records start here. The goal is simple: better information, fewer surprises, and cleaner results at year-end.

Who This Book Is For / Who It Is Not For

Who This Book Is For:
This workbook is designed for sole proprietors, single-member LLCs, independent contractors, freelancers, and other self-employed individuals who report business income and expenses on **IRS Schedule C**.

It is intended for business owners who want a practical, organized way to track expenses, mileage references, contractor payments, home office information, and year-end totals throughout the year.

Who This Book Is Not For:
This book is not intended for corporations, partnerships, or businesses filing returns other than Schedule C, nor is it a replacement for professional tax, legal, or payroll advice.

If your situation involves complex inventory accounting, employees, multiple entities, or international tax considerations, this workbook should be used only as a recordkeeping tool in coordination with a qualified professional.

How to Use This Book

This workbook is designed to help you organize business expenses quickly and accurately.

- Record each deductible expense in the appropriate category.
- Use the separate worksheets provided for:

  Home Office

  Self-Employed Health Insurance deductions.
- Use a separate Mileage Log for vehicle expenses and recording business mileage

Mileage Log Book Referral (Optional)

Vehicle mileage must be tracked separately.

Any mileage log used should meet IRS recordkeeping requirements.

Please refer to your dedicated Mileage Log Book for all mileage-related deductions.

Deluxe version Mileage Log Book Titles on Amazon for consideration with IRS compliance helps with separate sections for business, medical, charitable and volunteer mileage included authored by Amy Rose Herrick:

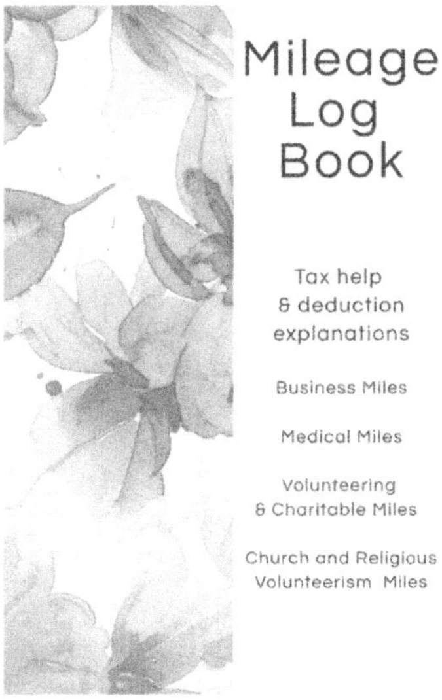

Basic version Mileage Log Book Titles on Amazon with only business mileage logs included authored by Amy Rose Herrick:

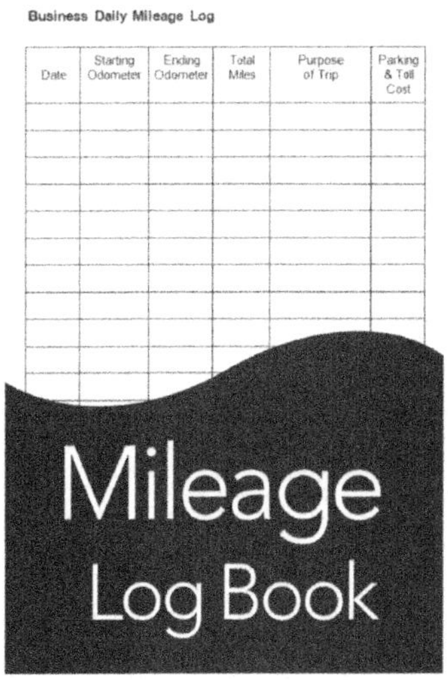

Schedule C Companion Reference (Optional)

For readers who want a clearer understanding of how Schedule C deductions work and what expense categories may apply to their business, you may find it helpful to reference *Self-Employed Taxes: Unleashing Schedule C Deductions*.

This companion book focuses on explaining the Schedule C form itself and how common deductions are treated under current tax law, while this record book is designed specifically for organizing and documenting your expenses. Used together, they can support better understanding and cleaner records.

IRS Category Definitions

Advertising: Costs for promoting your business such as flyers, business cards, and online ads.

Commissions and Fees: Payments made to non-employees for services provided.

Insurance: Business insurance premiums (excluding health).

Legal and Professional Services: Attorney fees, accounting fees, and consultant costs.

Office Expenses: Office supplies, postage, and small equipment under IRS thresholds.

Repairs and Maintenance: Upkeep of business property and equipment.

Supplies: Materials used in your business that are not included in inventory.

Taxes and Licenses: Business-related state, federal, and local taxes; permits and licenses.

Travel: Business travel expenses excluding meals.

Meals: Meals with clients or business-related meals (subject to IRS limits).

Utilities: Business portion of electricity, water, telecommunications, etc.

Sample Completed Entry

Date	1/13	1/19	1/10	1/15	1/15	1/15	1/19	
Vendor or Payee	Johnsons	Wallmart	Al Expo	AA	Marriott	RS DOL	Ofcmax	
Description	Laptop Repair	Office Supplies	Booth	June Air	June Hotel	License	Supplies	Page Total
Advertising			1500					$ 1,500.00
Commissions & Fees								
Employee Benefit Programs								
Insurance -Other								
Business Interest								
Legal & Professional Services								
Office Expenses		157.18					25.17	$ 182.35
Pension & Profit Sharing								
Rent or Lease								
Repairs & Maintenance	87.14							$ 87.14
Supplies								
Taxes & Licenses						250		$ 250.00
Travel				987.24	671.5			$ 1,658.74
Meals								
Business Utilities Only								
Miscellaneous								

Note #1:Home Office, Contractor payments, Depreciated Items and Self-Employed Health Insurance are summarized on dedicated pages a separate section of this book.

Note #2: Track your business miles and vehicle expenses in a separate mileage log to ensure accurate reporting and to determine the best deduction method for your situation.

Note #3: Cost of Goods is in another dedicated section of the book.

Note #4: I suggest you use a payroll program if you have employees that will require issuing a W2 for wages to ensure accurate reporting.

Date								
Vendor or Payee								
Description								Page Total
Advertising								
Commissions & Fees								
Employee Benefit Programs								
Insurance -Other								
Business Interest								
Legal & Professional Services								
Office Expenses								
Pension & Profit Sharing								
Rent or Lease								
Repairs & Maintenance								
Supplies								
Taxes & Licenses								
Travel								
Meals								
Business Utilities Only								
Miscellaneous								

Note #1:Home Office, Contractor payments, Depreciated Items and Self-Employed Health Insurance are summarized on dedicated pages a separate section of this book.

Note #2: Track your business miles and vehicle expenses in a separate mileage log to ensure accurate reporting and to determine the best deduction method for your situation.

Note #3: Cost of Goods is in another dedicated section of the book.

Note #4: I suggest you use a payroll program if you have employees that will require issuing a W2 for wages to ensure accurate reporting.

Date								
Vendor or Payee								
Description								Page Total
Advertising								
Commissions & Fees								
Employee Benefit Programs								
Insurance -Other								
Business Interest								
Legal & Professional Services								
Office Expenses								
Pension & Profit Sharing								
Rent or Lease								
Repairs & Maintenance								
Supplies								
Taxes & Licenses								
Travel								
Meals								
Business Utilities Only								
Miscellaneous								

Note #1:Home Office, Contractor payments, Depreciated Items and Self-Employed Health Insurance are summarized on dedicated pages a separate section of this book.

Note #2: Track your business miles and vehicle expenses in a separate mileage log to ensure accurate reporting and to determine the best deduction method for your situation.

Note #3: Cost of Goods is in another dedicated section of the book.

Note #4: I suggest you use a payroll program if you have employees that will require issuing a W2 for wages to ensure accurate reporting.

Date								
Vendor or Payee								
Description								Page Total
Advertising								
Commissions & Fees								
Employee Benefit Programs								
Insurance -Other								
Business Interest								
Legal & Professional Services								
Office Expenses								
Pension & Profit Sharing								
Rent or Lease								
Repairs & Maintenance								
Supplies								
Taxes & Licenses								
Travel								
Meals								
Business Utilities Only								
Miscellaneous								

Note #1:Home Office, Contractor payments, Depreciated Items and Self-Employed Health Insurance are summarized on dedicated pages a separate section of this book.

Note #2: Track your business miles and vehicle expenses in a separate mileage log to ensure accurate reporting and to determine the best deduction method for your situation.

Note #3: Cost of Goods is in another dedicated section of the book.

Note #4: I suggest you use a payroll program if you have employees that will require issuing a W2 for wages to ensure accurate reporting.

Date								
Vendor or Payee								
Description								Page Total
Advertising								
Commissions & Fees								
Employee Benefit Programs								
Insurance -Other								
Business Interest								
Legal & Professional Services								
Office Expenses								
Pension & Profit Sharing								
Rent or Lease								
Repairs & Maintenance								
Supplies								
Taxes & Licenses								
Travel								
Meals								
Business Utilities Only								
Miscellaneous								

Note #1:Home Office, Contractor payments, Depreciated Items and Self-Employed Health Insurance are summarized on dedicated pages a separate section of this book.

Note #2: Track your business miles and vehicle expenses in a separate mileage log to ensure accurate reporting and to determine the best deduction method for your situation.

Note #3: Cost of Goods is in another dedicated section of the book.

Note #4: I suggest you use a payroll program if you have employees that will require issuing a W2 for wages to ensure accurate reporting.

Date								
Vendor or Payee								
Description								Page Total
Advertising								
Commissions & Fees								
Employee Benefit Programs								
Insurance -Other								
Business Interest								
Legal & Professional Services								
Office Expenses								
Pension & Profit Sharing								
Rent or Lease								
Repairs & Maintenance								
Supplies								
Taxes & Licenses								
Travel								
Meals								
Business Utilities Only								
Miscellaneous								

Note #1:Home Office, Contractor payments, Depreciated Items and Self-Employed Health Insurance are summarized on dedicated pages a separate section of this book.

Note #2: Track your business miles and vehicle expenses in a separate mileage log to ensure accurate reporting and to determine the best deduction method for your situation.

Note #3: Cost of Goods is in another dedicated section of the book.

Note #4: I suggest you use a payroll program if you have employees that will require issuing a W2 for wages to ensure accurate reporting.

Date								
Vendor or Payee								
Description								Page Total
Advertising								
Commissions & Fees								
Employee Benefit Programs								
Insurance -Other								
Business Interest								
Legal & Professional Services								
Office Expenses								
Pension & Profit Sharing								
Rent or Lease								
Repairs & Maintenance								
Supplies								
Taxes & Licenses								
Travel								
Meals								
Business Utilities Only								
Miscellaneous								

Note #1:Home Office, Contractor payments, Depreciated Items and Self-Employed Health Insurance are summarized on dedicated pages a separate section of this book.

Note #2: Track your business miles and vehicle expenses in a separate mileage log to ensure accurate reporting and to determine the best deduction method for your situation.

Note #3: Cost of Goods is in another dedicated section of the book.

Note #4: I suggest you use a payroll program if you have employees that will require issuing a W2 for wages to ensure accurate reporting.

Date								
Vendor or Payee								
Description								Page Total
Advertising								
Commissions & Fees								
Employee Benefit Programs								
Insurance -Other								
Business Interest								
Legal & Professional Services								
Office Expenses								
Pension & Profit Sharing								
Rent or Lease								
Repairs & Maintenance								
Supplies								
Taxes & Licenses								
Travel								
Meals								
Business Utilities Only								
Miscellaneous								

Note #1:Home Office, Contractor payments, Depreciated Items and Self-Employed Health Insurance are summarized on dedicated pages a separate section of this book.

Note #2: Track your business miles and vehicle expenses in a separate mileage log to ensure accurate reporting and to determine the best deduction method for your situation.

Note #3: Cost of Goods is in another dedicated section of the book.

Note #4: I suggest you use a payroll program if you have employees that will require issuing a W2 for wages to ensure accurate reporting.

Date								
Vendor or Payee								
Description								Page Total
Advertising								
Commissions & Fees								
Employee Benefit Programs								
Insurance -Other								
Business Interest								
Legal & Professional Services								
Office Expenses								
Pension & Profit Sharing								
Rent or Lease								
Repairs & Maintenance								
Supplies								
Taxes & Licenses								
Travel								
Meals								
Business Utilities Only								
Miscellaneous								

Note #1:Home Office, Contractor payments, Depreciated Items and Self-Employed Health Insurance are summarized on dedicated pages a separate section of this book.

Note #2: Track your business miles and vehicle expenses in a separate mileage log to ensure accurate reporting and to determine the best deduction method for your situation.

Note #3: Cost of Goods is in another dedicated section of the book.

Note #4: I suggest you use a payroll program if you have employees that will require issuing a W2 for wages to ensure accurate reporting.

Date								
Vendor or Payee								
Description								Page Total
Advertising								
Commissions & Fees								
Employee Benefit Programs								
Insurance -Other								
Business Interest								
Legal & Professional Services								
Office Expenses								
Pension & Profit Sharing								
Rent or Lease								
Repairs & Maintenance								
Supplies								
Taxes & Licenses								
Travel								
Meals								
Business Utilities Only								
Miscellaneous								

Note #1:Home Office, Contractor payments, Depreciated Items and Self-Employed Health Insurance are summarized on dedicated pages a separate section of this book.

Note #2: Track your business miles and vehicle expenses in a separate mileage log to ensure accurate reporting and to determine the best deduction method for your situation.

Note #3: Cost of Goods is in another dedicated section of the book.

Note #4: I suggest you use a payroll program if you have employees that will require issuing a W2 for wages to ensure accurate reporting.

Date								
Vendor or Payee								
Description								Page Total
Advertising								
Commissions & Fees								
Employee Benefit Programs								
Insurance -Other								
Business Interest								
Legal & Professional Services								
Office Expenses								
Pension & Profit Sharing								
Rent or Lease								
Repairs & Maintenance								
Supplies								
Taxes & Licenses								
Travel								
Meals								
Business Utilities Only								
Miscellaneous								

Note #1:Home Office, Contractor payments, Depreciated Items and Self-Employed Health Insurance are summarized on dedicated pages a separate section of this book.

Note #2: Track your business miles and vehicle expenses in a separate mileage log to ensure accurate reporting and to determine the best deduction method for your situation.

Note #3: Cost of Goods is in another dedicated section of the book.

Note #4: I suggest you use a payroll program if you have employees that will require issuing a W2 for wages to ensure accurate reporting.

Date								
Vendor or Payee								
Description								Page Total
Advertising								
Commissions & Fees								
Employee Benefit Programs								
Insurance -Other								
Business Interest								
Legal & Professional Services								
Office Expenses								
Pension & Profit Sharing								
Rent or Lease								
Repairs & Maintenance								
Supplies								
Taxes & Licenses								
Travel								
Meals								
Business Utilities Only								
Miscellaneous								

Note #1:Home Office, Contractor payments, Depreciated Items and Self-Employed Health Insurance are summarized on dedicated pages a separate section of this book.

Note #2: Track your business miles and vehicle expenses in a separate mileage log to ensure accurate reporting and to determine the best deduction method for your situation.

Note #3: Cost of Goods is in another dedicated section of the book.

Note #4: I suggest you use a payroll program if you have employees that will require issuing a W2 for wages to ensure accurate reporting.

Date								
Vendor or Payee								
Description								Page Total
Advertising								
Commissions & Fees								
Employee Benefit Programs								
Insurance -Other								
Business Interest								
Legal & Professional Services								
Office Expenses								
Pension & Profit Sharing								
Rent or Lease								
Repairs & Maintenance								
Supplies								
Taxes & Licenses								
Travel								
Meals								
Business Utilities Only								
Miscellaneous								

Note #1:Home Office, Contractor payments, Depreciated Items and Self-Employed Health Insurance are summarized on dedicated pages a separate section of this book.

Note #2: Track your business miles and vehicle expenses in a separate mileage log to ensure accurate reporting and to determine the best deduction method for your situation.

Note #3: Cost of Goods is in another dedicated section of the book.

Note #4: I suggest you use a payroll program if you have employees that will require issuing a W2 for wages to ensure accurate reporting.

Date								
Vendor or Payee								
Description								Page Total
Advertising								
Commissions & Fees								
Employee Benefit Programs								
Insurance -Other								
Business Interest								
Legal & Professional Services								
Office Expenses								
Pension & Profit Sharing								
Rent or Lease								
Repairs & Maintenance								
Supplies								
Taxes & Licenses								
Travel								
Meals								
Business Utilities Only								
Miscellaneous								

Note #1:Home Office, Contractor payments, Depreciated Items and Self-Employed Health Insurance are summarized on dedicated pages a separate section of this book.

Note #2: Track your business miles and vehicle expenses in a separate mileage log to ensure accurate reporting and to determine the best deduction method for your situation.

Note #3: Cost of Goods is in another dedicated section of the book.

Note #4: I suggest you use a payroll program if you have employees that will require issuing a W2 for wages to ensure accurate reporting.

Date								
Vendor or Payee								
Description								Page Total
Advertising								
Commissions & Fees								
Employee Benefit Programs								
Insurance -Other								
Business Interest								
Legal & Professional Services								
Office Expenses								
Pension & Profit Sharing								
Rent or Lease								
Repairs & Maintenance								
Supplies								
Taxes & Licenses								
Travel								
Meals								
Business Utilities Only								
Miscellaneous								

Note #1:Home Office, Contractor payments, Depreciated Items and Self-Employed Health Insurance are summarized on dedicated pages a separate section of this book.

Note #2: Track your business miles and vehicle expenses in a separate mileage log to ensure accurate reporting and to determine the best deduction method for your situation.

Note #3: Cost of Goods is in another dedicated section of the book.

Note #4: I suggest you use a payroll program if you have employees that will require issuing a W2 for wages to ensure accurate reporting.

Date								
Vendor or Payee								
Description								Page Total
Advertising								
Commissions & Fees								
Employee Benefit Programs								
Insurance -Other								
Business Interest								
Legal & Professional Services								
Office Expenses								
Pension & Profit Sharing								
Rent or Lease								
Repairs & Maintenance								
Supplies								
Taxes & Licenses								
Travel								
Meals								
Business Utilities Only								
Miscellaneous								

Note #1:Home Office, Contractor payments, Depreciated Items and Self-Employed Health Insurance are summarized on dedicated pages a separate section of this book.

Note #2: Track your business miles and vehicle expenses in a separate mileage log to ensure accurate reporting and to determine the best deduction method for your situation.

Note #3: Cost of Goods is in another dedicated section of the book.

Note #4: I suggest you use a payroll program if you have employees that will require issuing a W2 for wages to ensure accurate reporting.

Date								
Vendor or Payee								
Description								Page Total
Advertising								
Commissions & Fees								
Employee Benefit Programs								
Insurance -Other								
Business Interest								
Legal & Professional Services								
Office Expenses								
Pension & Profit Sharing								
Rent or Lease								
Repairs & Maintenance								
Supplies								
Taxes & Licenses								
Travel								
Meals								
Business Utilities Only								
Miscellaneous								

Note #1:Home Office, Contractor payments, Depreciated Items and Self-Employed Health Insurance are summarized on dedicated pages a separate section of this book.

Note #2: Track your business miles and vehicle expenses in a separate mileage log to ensure accurate reporting and to determine the best deduction method for your situation.

Note #3: Cost of Goods is in another dedicated section of the book.

Note #4: I suggest you use a payroll program if you have employees that will require issuing a W2 for wages to ensure accurate reporting.

Date								
Vendor or Payee								
Description								Page Total
Advertising								
Commissions & Fees								
Employee Benefit Programs								
Insurance -Other								
Business Interest								
Legal & Professional Services								
Office Expenses								
Pension & Profit Sharing								
Rent or Lease								
Repairs & Maintenance								
Supplies								
Taxes & Licenses								
Travel								
Meals								
Business Utilities Only								
Miscellaneous								

Note #1:Home Office, Contractor payments, Depreciated Items and Self-Employed Health Insurance are summarized on dedicated pages a separate section of this book.

Note #2: Track your business miles and vehicle expenses in a separate mileage log to ensure accurate reporting and to determine the best deduction method for your situation.

Note #3: Cost of Goods is in another dedicated section of the book.

Note #4: I suggest you use a payroll program if you have employees that will require issuing a W2 for wages to ensure accurate reporting.

Date								
Vendor or Payee								
Description								Page Total
Advertising								
Commissions & Fees								
Employee Benefit Programs								
Insurance -Other								
Business Interest								
Legal & Professional Services								
Office Expenses								
Pension & Profit Sharing								
Rent or Lease								
Repairs & Maintenance								
Supplies								
Taxes & Licenses								
Travel								
Meals								
Business Utilities Only								
Miscellaneous								

Note #1:Home Office, Contractor payments, Depreciated Items and Self-Employed Health Insurance are summarized on dedicated pages a separate section of this book.

Note #2: Track your business miles and vehicle expenses in a separate mileage log to ensure accurate reporting and to determine the best deduction method for your situation.

Note #3: Cost of Goods is in another dedicated section of the book.

Note #4: I suggest you use a payroll program if you have employees that will require issuing a W2 for wages to ensure accurate reporting.

Date								
Vendor or Payee								
Description								Page Total
Advertising								
Commissions & Fees								
Employee Benefit Programs								
Insurance -Other								
Business Interest								
Legal & Professional Services								
Office Expenses								
Pension & Profit Sharing								
Rent or Lease								
Repairs & Maintenance								
Supplies								
Taxes & Licenses								
Travel								
Meals								
Business Utilities Only								
Miscellaneous								

Note #1:Home Office, Contractor payments, Depreciated Items and Self-Employed Health Insurance are summarized on dedicated pages a separate section of this book.

Note #2: Track your business miles and vehicle expenses in a separate mileage log to ensure accurate reporting and to determine the best deduction method for your situation.

Note #3: Cost of Goods is in another dedicated section of the book.

Note #4: I suggest you use a payroll program if you have employees that will require issuing a W2 for wages to ensure accurate reporting.

Date								
Vendor or Payee								
Description								Page Total
Advertising								
Commissions & Fees								
Employee Benefit Programs								
Insurance -Other								
Business Interest								
Legal & Professional Services								
Office Expenses								
Pension & Profit Sharing								
Rent or Lease								
Repairs & Maintenance								
Supplies								
Taxes & Licenses								
Travel								
Meals								
Business Utilities Only								
Miscellaneous								

Note #1:Home Office, Contractor payments, Depreciated Items and Self-Employed Health Insurance are summarized on dedicated pages a separate section of this book.

Note #2: Track your business miles and vehicle expenses in a separate mileage log to ensure accurate reporting and to determine the best deduction method for your situation.

Note #3: Cost of Goods is in another dedicated section of the book.

Note #4: I suggest you use a payroll program if you have employees that will require issuing a W2 for wages to ensure accurate reporting.

Date								
Vendor or Payee								
Description								Page Total
Advertising								
Commissions & Fees								
Employee Benefit Programs								
Insurance -Other								
Business Interest								
Legal & Professional Services								
Office Expenses								
Pension & Profit Sharing								
Rent or Lease								
Repairs & Maintenance								
Supplies								
Taxes & Licenses								
Travel								
Meals								
Business Utilities Only								
Miscellaneous								

Note #1:Home Office, Contractor payments, Depreciated Items and Self-Employed Health Insurance are summarized on dedicated pages a separate section of this book.

Note #2: Track your business miles and vehicle expenses in a separate mileage log to ensure accurate reporting and to determine the best deduction method for your situation.

Note #3: Cost of Goods is in another dedicated section of the book.

Note #4: I suggest you use a payroll program if you have employees that will require issuing a W2 for wages to ensure accurate reporting.

Date								
Vendor or Payee								
Description								Page Total
Advertising								
Commissions & Fees								
Employee Benefit Programs								
Insurance -Other								
Business Interest								
Legal & Professional Services								
Office Expenses								
Pension & Profit Sharing								
Rent or Lease								
Repairs & Maintenance								
Supplies								
Taxes & Licenses								
Travel								
Meals								
Business Utilities Only								
Miscellaneous								

Note #1:Home Office, Contractor payments, Depreciated Items and Self-Employed Health Insurance are summarized on dedicated pages a separate section of this book.

Note #2: Track your business miles and vehicle expenses in a separate mileage log to ensure accurate reporting and to determine the best deduction method for your situation.

Note #3: Cost of Goods is in another dedicated section of the book.

Note #4: I suggest you use a payroll program if you have employees that will require issuing a W2 for wages to ensure accurate reporting.

Date								
Vendor or Payee								
Description								Page Total
Advertising								
Commissions & Fees								
Employee Benefit Programs								
Insurance -Other								
Business Interest								
Legal & Professional Services								
Office Expenses								
Pension & Profit Sharing								
Rent or Lease								
Repairs & Maintenance								
Supplies								
Taxes & Licenses								
Travel								
Meals								
Business Utilities Only								
Miscellaneous								

Note #1:Home Office, Contractor payments, Depreciated Items and Self-Employed Health Insurance are summarized on dedicated pages a separate section of this book.

Note #2: Track your business miles and vehicle expenses in a separate mileage log to ensure accurate reporting and to determine the best deduction method for your situation.

Note #3: Cost of Goods is in another dedicated section of the book.

Note #4: I suggest you use a payroll program if you have employees that will require issuing a W2 for wages to ensure accurate reporting.

Date								
Vendor or Payee								
Description								Page Total
Advertising								
Commissions & Fees								
Employee Benefit Programs								
Insurance -Other								
Business Interest								
Legal & Professional Services								
Office Expenses								
Pension & Profit Sharing								
Rent or Lease								
Repairs & Maintenance								
Supplies								
Taxes & Licenses								
Travel								
Meals								
Business Utilities Only								
Miscellaneous								

Note #1:Home Office, Contractor payments, Depreciated Items and Self-Employed Health Insurance are summarized on dedicated pages a separate section of this book.

Note #2: Track your business miles and vehicle expenses in a separate mileage log to ensure accurate reporting and to determine the best deduction method for your situation.

Note #3: Cost of Goods is in another dedicated section of the book.

Note #4: I suggest you use a payroll program if you have employees that will require issuing a W2 for wages to ensure accurate reporting.

Date								
Vendor or Payee								
Description								Page Total
Advertising								
Commissions & Fees								
Employee Benefit Programs								
Insurance -Other								
Business Interest								
Legal & Professional Services								
Office Expenses								
Pension & Profit Sharing								
Rent or Lease								
Repairs & Maintenance								
Supplies								
Taxes & Licenses								
Travel								
Meals								
Business Utilities Only								
Miscellaneous								

Note #1:Home Office, Contractor payments, Depreciated Items and Self-Employed Health Insurance are summarized on dedicated pages a separate section of this book.

Note #2: Track your business miles and vehicle expenses in a separate mileage log to ensure accurate reporting and to determine the best deduction method for your situation.

Note #3: Cost of Goods is in another dedicated section of the book.

Note #4: I suggest you use a payroll program if you have employees that will require issuing a W2 for wages to ensure accurate reporting.

Date								
Vendor or Payee								
Description								Page Total
Advertising								
Commissions & Fees								
Employee Benefit Programs								
Insurance -Other								
Business Interest								
Legal & Professional Services								
Office Expenses								
Pension & Profit Sharing								
Rent or Lease								
Repairs & Maintenance								
Supplies								
Taxes & Licenses								
Travel								
Meals								
Business Utilities Only								
Miscellaneous								

Note #1:Home Office, Contractor payments, Depreciated Items and Self-Employed Health Insurance are summarized on dedicated pages a separate section of this book.

Note #2: Track your business miles and vehicle expenses in a separate mileage log to ensure accurate reporting and to determine the best deduction method for your situation.

Note #3: Cost of Goods is in another dedicated section of the book.

Note #4: I suggest you use a payroll program if you have employees that will require issuing a W2 for wages to ensure accurate reporting.

Date								
Vendor or Payee								
Description								Page Total
Advertising								
Commissions & Fees								
Employee Benefit Programs								
Insurance -Other								
Business Interest								
Legal & Professional Services								
Office Expenses								
Pension & Profit Sharing								
Rent or Lease								
Repairs & Maintenance								
Supplies								
Taxes & Licenses								
Travel								
Meals								
Business Utilities Only								
Miscellaneous								

Note #1:Home Office, Contractor payments, Depreciated Items and Self-Employed Health Insurance are summarized on dedicated pages a separate section of this book.

Note #2: Track your business miles and vehicle expenses in a separate mileage log to ensure accurate reporting and to determine the best deduction method for your situation.

Note #3: Cost of Goods is in another dedicated section of the book.

Note #4: I suggest you use a payroll program if you have employees that will require issuing a W2 for wages to ensure accurate reporting.

Date								
Vendor or Payee								
Description								Page Total
Advertising								
Commissions & Fees								
Employee Benefit Programs								
Insurance -Other								
Business Interest								
Legal & Professional Services								
Office Expenses								
Pension & Profit Sharing								
Rent or Lease								
Repairs & Maintenance								
Supplies								
Taxes & Licenses								
Travel								
Meals								
Business Utilities Only								
Miscellaneous								

Note #1:Home Office, Contractor payments, Depreciated Items and Self-Employed Health Insurance are summarized on dedicated pages a separate section of this book.

Note #2: Track your business miles and vehicle expenses in a separate mileage log to ensure accurate reporting and to determine the best deduction method for your situation.

Note #3: Cost of Goods is in another dedicated section of the book.

Note #4: I suggest you use a payroll program if you have employees that will require issuing a W2 for wages to ensure accurate reporting.

Date								
Vendor or Payee								
Description								Page Total
Advertising								
Commissions & Fees								
Employee Benefit Programs								
Insurance -Other								
Business Interest								
Legal & Professional Services								
Office Expenses								
Pension & Profit Sharing								
Rent or Lease								
Repairs & Maintenance								
Supplies								
Taxes & Licenses								
Travel								
Meals								
Business Utilities Only								
Miscellaneous								

Note #1:Home Office, Contractor payments, Depreciated Items and Self-Employed Health Insurance are summarized on dedicated pages a separate section of this book.

Note #2: Track your business miles and vehicle expenses in a separate mileage log to ensure accurate reporting and to determine the best deduction method for your situation.

Note #3: Cost of Goods is in another dedicated section of the book.

Note #4: I suggest you use a payroll program if you have employees that will require issuing a W2 for wages to ensure accurate reporting.

Date								
Vendor or Payee								
Description								Page Total
Advertising								
Commissions & Fees								
Employee Benefit Programs								
Insurance -Other								
Business Interest								
Legal & Professional Services								
Office Expenses								
Pension & Profit Sharing								
Rent or Lease								
Repairs & Maintenance								
Supplies								
Taxes & Licenses								
Travel								
Meals								
Business Utilities Only								
Miscellaneous								

Note #1:Home Office, Contractor payments, Depreciated Items and Self-Employed Health Insurance are summarized on dedicated pages a separate section of this book.

Note #2: Track your business miles and vehicle expenses in a separate mileage log to ensure accurate reporting and to determine the best deduction method for your situation.

Note #3: Cost of Goods is in another dedicated section of the book.

Note #4: I suggest you use a payroll program if you have employees that will require issuing a W2 for wages to ensure accurate reporting.

Date								
Vendor or Payee								
Description								Page Total
Advertising								
Commissions & Fees								
Employee Benefit Programs								
Insurance -Other								
Business Interest								
Legal & Professional Services								
Office Expenses								
Pension & Profit Sharing								
Rent or Lease								
Repairs & Maintenance								
Supplies								
Taxes & Licenses								
Travel								
Meals								
Business Utilities Only								
Miscellaneous								

Note #1:Home Office, Contractor payments, Depreciated Items and Self-Employed Health Insurance are summarized on dedicated pages a separate section of this book.

Note #2: Track your business miles and vehicle expenses in a separate mileage log to ensure accurate reporting and to determine the best deduction method for your situation.

Note #3: Cost of Goods is in another dedicated section of the book.

Note #4: I suggest you use a payroll program if you have employees that will require issuing a W2 for wages to ensure accurate reporting.

Date								
Vendor or Payee								
Description								Page Total
Advertising								
Commissions & Fees								
Employee Benefit Programs								
Insurance -Other								
Business Interest								
Legal & Professional Services								
Office Expenses								
Pension & Profit Sharing								
Rent or Lease								
Repairs & Maintenance								
Supplies								
Taxes & Licenses								
Travel								
Meals								
Business Utilities Only								
Miscellaneous								

Note #1:Home Office, Contractor payments, Depreciated Items and Self-Employed Health Insurance are summarized on dedicated pages a separate section of this book.

Note #2: Track your business miles and vehicle expenses in a separate mileage log to ensure accurate reporting and to determine the best deduction method for your situation.

Note #3: Cost of Goods is in another dedicated section of the book.

Note #4: I suggest you use a payroll program if you have employees that will require issuing a W2 for wages to ensure accurate reporting.

Date								
Vendor or Payee								
Description								Page Total
Advertising								
Commissions & Fees								
Employee Benefit Programs								
Insurance -Other								
Business Interest								
Legal & Professional Services								
Office Expenses								
Pension & Profit Sharing								
Rent or Lease								
Repairs & Maintenance								
Supplies								
Taxes & Licenses								
Travel								
Meals								
Business Utilities Only								
Miscellaneous								

Note #1:Home Office, Contractor payments, Depreciated Items and Self-Employed Health Insurance are summarized on dedicated pages a separate section of this book.

Note #2: Track your business miles and vehicle expenses in a separate mileage log to ensure accurate reporting and to determine the best deduction method for your situation.

Note #3: Cost of Goods is in another dedicated section of the book.

Note #4: I suggest you use a payroll program if you have employees that will require issuing a W2 for wages to ensure accurate reporting.

Date								
Vendor or Payee								
Description								Page Total
Advertising								
Commissions & Fees								
Employee Benefit Programs								
Insurance -Other								
Business Interest								
Legal & Professional Services								
Office Expenses								
Pension & Profit Sharing								
Rent or Lease								
Repairs & Maintenance								
Supplies								
Taxes & Licenses								
Travel								
Meals								
Business Utilities Only								
Miscellaneous								

Note #1:Home Office, Contractor payments, Depreciated Items and Self-Employed Health Insurance are summarized on dedicated pages a separate section of this book.

Note #2: Track your business miles and vehicle expenses in a separate mileage log to ensure accurate reporting and to determine the best deduction method for your situation.

Note #3: Cost of Goods is in another dedicated section of the book.

Note #4: I suggest you use a payroll program if you have employees that will require issuing a W2 for wages to ensure accurate reporting.

Date								
Vendor or Payee								
Description								Page Total
Advertising								
Commissions & Fees								
Employee Benefit Programs								
Insurance -Other								
Business Interest								
Legal & Professional Services								
Office Expenses								
Pension & Profit Sharing								
Rent or Lease								
Repairs & Maintenance								
Supplies								
Taxes & Licenses								
Travel								
Meals								
Business Utilities Only								
Miscellaneous								

Note #1:Home Office, Contractor payments, Depreciated Items and Self-Employed Health Insurance are summarized on dedicated pages a separate section of this book.

Note #2: Track your business miles and vehicle expenses in a separate mileage log to ensure accurate reporting and to determine the best deduction method for your situation.

Note #3: Cost of Goods is in another dedicated section of the book.

Note #4: I suggest you use a payroll program if you have employees that will require issuing a W2 for wages to ensure accurate reporting.

Date								
Vendor or Payee								
Description								Page Total
Advertising								
Commissions & Fees								
Employee Benefit Programs								
Insurance -Other								
Business Interest								
Legal & Professional Services								
Office Expenses								
Pension & Profit Sharing								
Rent or Lease								
Repairs & Maintenance								
Supplies								
Taxes & Licenses								
Travel								
Meals								
Business Utilities Only								
Miscellaneous								

Note #1:Home Office, Contractor payments, Depreciated Items and Self-Employed Health Insurance are summarized on dedicated pages a separate section of this book.

Note #2: Track your business miles and vehicle expenses in a separate mileage log to ensure accurate reporting and to determine the best deduction method for your situation.

Note #3: Cost of Goods is in another dedicated section of the book.

Note #4: I suggest you use a payroll program if you have employees that will require issuing a W2 for wages to ensure accurate reporting.

Date								
Vendor or Payee								
Description								Page Total
Advertising								
Commissions & Fees								
Employee Benefit Programs								
Insurance -Other								
Business Interest								
Legal & Professional Services								
Office Expenses								
Pension & Profit Sharing								
Rent or Lease								
Repairs & Maintenance								
Supplies								
Taxes & Licenses								
Travel								
Meals								
Business Utilities Only								
Miscellaneous								

Note #1:Home Office, Contractor payments, Depreciated Items and Self-Employed Health Insurance are summarized on dedicated pages a separate section of this book.

Note #2: Track your business miles and vehicle expenses in a separate mileage log to ensure accurate reporting and to determine the best deduction method for your situation.

Note #3: Cost of Goods is in another dedicated section of the book.

Note #4: I suggest you use a payroll program if you have employees that will require issuing a W2 for wages to ensure accurate reporting.

Date								
Vendor or Payee								
Description								Page Total
Advertising								
Commissions & Fees								
Employee Benefit Programs								
Insurance -Other								
Business Interest								
Legal & Professional Services								
Office Expenses								
Pension & Profit Sharing								
Rent or Lease								
Repairs & Maintenance								
Supplies								
Taxes & Licenses								
Travel								
Meals								
Business Utilities Only								
Miscellaneous								

Note #1:Home Office, Contractor payments, Depreciated Items and Self-Employed Health Insurance are summarized on dedicated pages a separate section of this book.

Note #2: Track your business miles and vehicle expenses in a separate mileage log to ensure accurate reporting and to determine the best deduction method for your situation.

Note #3: Cost of Goods is in another dedicated section of the book.

Note #4: I suggest you use a payroll program if you have employees that will require issuing a W2 for wages to ensure accurate reporting.

Date								
Vendor or Payee								
Description								Page Total
Advertising								
Commissions & Fees								
Employee Benefit Programs								
Insurance -Other								
Business Interest								
Legal & Professional Services								
Office Expenses								
Pension & Profit Sharing								
Rent or Lease								
Repairs & Maintenance								
Supplies								
Taxes & Licenses								
Travel								
Meals								
Business Utilities Only								
Miscellaneous								

Note #1:Home Office, Contractor payments, Depreciated Items and Self-Employed Health Insurance are summarized on dedicated pages a separate section of this book.

Note #2: Track your business miles and vehicle expenses in a separate mileage log to ensure accurate reporting and to determine the best deduction method for your situation.

Note #3: Cost of Goods is in another dedicated section of the book.

Note #4: I suggest you use a payroll program if you have employees that will require issuing a W2 for wages to ensure accurate reporting.

Date								
Vendor or Payee								
Description								Page Total
Advertising								
Commissions & Fees								
Employee Benefit Programs								
Insurance -Other								
Business Interest								
Legal & Professional Services								
Office Expenses								
Pension & Profit Sharing								
Rent or Lease								
Repairs & Maintenance								
Supplies								
Taxes & Licenses								
Travel								
Meals								
Business Utilities Only								
Miscellaneous								

Note #1:Home Office, Contractor payments, Depreciated Items and Self-Employed Health Insurance are summarized on dedicated pages a separate section of this book.

Note #2: Track your business miles and vehicle expenses in a separate mileage log to ensure accurate reporting and to determine the best deduction method for your situation.

Note #3: Cost of Goods is in another dedicated section of the book.

Note #4: I suggest you use a payroll program if you have employees that will require issuing a W2 for wages to ensure accurate reporting.

Date								
Vendor or Payee								
Description								Page Total
Advertising								
Commissions & Fees								
Employee Benefit Programs								
Insurance -Other								
Business Interest								
Legal & Professional Services								
Office Expenses								
Pension & Profit Sharing								
Rent or Lease								
Repairs & Maintenance								
Supplies								
Taxes & Licenses								
Travel								
Meals								
Business Utilities Only								
Miscellaneous								

Note #1:Home Office, Contractor payments, Depreciated Items and Self-Employed Health Insurance are summarized on dedicated pages a separate section of this book.

Note #2: Track your business miles and vehicle expenses in a separate mileage log to ensure accurate reporting and to determine the best deduction method for your situation.

Note #3: Cost of Goods is in another dedicated section of the book.

Note #4: I suggest you use a payroll program if you have employees that will require issuing a W2 for wages to ensure accurate reporting.

Date								
Vendor or Payee								
Description								Page Total
Advertising								
Commissions & Fees								
Employee Benefit Programs								
Insurance -Other								
Business Interest								
Legal & Professional Services								
Office Expenses								
Pension & Profit Sharing								
Rent or Lease								
Repairs & Maintenance								
Supplies								
Taxes & Licenses								
Travel								
Meals								
Business Utilities Only								
Miscellaneous								

Note #1:Home Office, Contractor payments, Depreciated Items and Self-Employed Health Insurance are summarized on dedicated pages a separate section of this book.

Note #2: Track your business miles and vehicle expenses in a separate mileage log to ensure accurate reporting and to determine the best deduction method for your situation.

Note #3: Cost of Goods is in another dedicated section of the book.

Note #4: I suggest you use a payroll program if you have employees that will require issuing a W2 for wages to ensure accurate reporting.

Date								
Vendor or Payee								
Description								Page Total
Advertising								
Commissions & Fees								
Employee Benefit Programs								
Insurance -Other								
Business Interest								
Legal & Professional Services								
Office Expenses								
Pension & Profit Sharing								
Rent or Lease								
Repairs & Maintenance								
Supplies								
Taxes & Licenses								
Travel								
Meals								
Business Utilities Only								
Miscellaneous								

Note #1:Home Office, Contractor payments, Depreciated Items and Self-Employed Health Insurance are summarized on dedicated pages a separate section of this book.

Note #2: Track your business miles and vehicle expenses in a separate mileage log to ensure accurate reporting and to determine the best deduction method for your situation.

Note #3: Cost of Goods is in another dedicated section of the book.

Note #4: I suggest you use a payroll program if you have employees that will require issuing a W2 for wages to ensure accurate reporting.

Date								
Vendor or Payee								
Description								Page Total
Advertising								
Commissions & Fees								
Employee Benefit Programs								
Insurance -Other								
Business Interest								
Legal & Professional Services								
Office Expenses								
Pension & Profit Sharing								
Rent or Lease								
Repairs & Maintenance								
Supplies								
Taxes & Licenses								
Travel								
Meals								
Business Utilities Only								
Miscellaneous								

Note #1:Home Office, Contractor payments, Depreciated Items and Self-Employed Health Insurance are summarized on dedicated pages a separate section of this book.

Note #2: Track your business miles and vehicle expenses in a separate mileage log to ensure accurate reporting and to determine the best deduction method for your situation.

Note #3: Cost of Goods is in another dedicated section of the book.

Note #4: I suggest you use a payroll program if you have employees that will require issuing a W2 for wages to ensure accurate reporting.

Date								
Vendor or Payee								
Description								Page Total
Advertising								
Commissions & Fees								
Employee Benefit Programs								
Insurance -Other								
Business Interest								
Legal & Professional Services								
Office Expenses								
Pension & Profit Sharing								
Rent or Lease								
Repairs & Maintenance								
Supplies								
Taxes & Licenses								
Travel								
Meals								
Business Utilities Only								
Miscellaneous								

Note #1:Home Office, Contractor payments, Depreciated Items and Self-Employed Health Insurance are summarized on dedicated pages a separate section of this book.

Note #2: Track your business miles and vehicle expenses in a separate mileage log to ensure accurate reporting and to determine the best deduction method for your situation.

Note #3: Cost of Goods is in another dedicated section of the book.

Note #4: I suggest you use a payroll program if you have employees that will require issuing a W2 for wages to ensure accurate reporting.

Date								
Vendor or Payee								
Description								Page Total
Advertising								
Commissions & Fees								
Employee Benefit Programs								
Insurance -Other								
Business Interest								
Legal & Professional Services								
Office Expenses								
Pension & Profit Sharing								
Rent or Lease								
Repairs & Maintenance								
Supplies								
Taxes & Licenses								
Travel								
Meals								
Business Utilities Only								
Miscellaneous								

Note #1:Home Office, Contractor payments, Depreciated Items and Self-Employed Health Insurance are summarized on dedicated pages a separate section of this book.

Note #2: Track your business miles and vehicle expenses in a separate mileage log to ensure accurate reporting and to determine the best deduction method for your situation.

Note #3: Cost of Goods is in another dedicated section of the book.

Note #4: I suggest you use a payroll program if you have employees that will require issuing a W2 for wages to ensure accurate reporting.

Date								
Vendor or Payee								
Description								Page Total
Advertising								
Commissions & Fees								
Employee Benefit Programs								
Insurance -Other								
Business Interest								
Legal & Professional Services								
Office Expenses								
Pension & Profit Sharing								
Rent or Lease								
Repairs & Maintenance								
Supplies								
Taxes & Licenses								
Travel								
Meals								
Business Utilities Only								
Miscellaneous								

Note #1:Home Office, Contractor payments, Depreciated Items and Self-Employed Health Insurance are summarized on dedicated pages a separate section of this book.

Note #2: Track your business miles and vehicle expenses in a separate mileage log to ensure accurate reporting and to determine the best deduction method for your situation.

Note #3: Cost of Goods is in another dedicated section of the book.

Note #4: I suggest you use a payroll program if you have employees that will require issuing a W2 for wages to ensure accurate reporting.

Date								
Vendor or Payee								
Description								Page Total
Advertising								
Commissions & Fees								
Employee Benefit Programs								
Insurance -Other								
Business Interest								
Legal & Professional Services								
Office Expenses								
Pension & Profit Sharing								
Rent or Lease								
Repairs & Maintenance								
Supplies								
Taxes & Licenses								
Travel								
Meals								
Business Utilities Only								
Miscellaneous								

Note #1:Home Office, Contractor payments, Depreciated Items and Self-Employed Health Insurance are summarized on dedicated pages a separate section of this book.

Note #2: Track your business miles and vehicle expenses in a separate mileage log to ensure accurate reporting and to determine the best deduction method for your situation.

Note #3: Cost of Goods is in another dedicated section of the book.

Note #4: I suggest you use a payroll program if you have employees that will require issuing a W2 for wages to ensure accurate reporting.

Date								
Vendor or Payee								
Description								Page Total
Advertising								
Commissions & Fees								
Employee Benefit Programs								
Insurance -Other								
Business Interest								
Legal & Professional Services								
Office Expenses								
Pension & Profit Sharing								
Rent or Lease								
Repairs & Maintenance								
Supplies								
Taxes & Licenses								
Travel								
Meals								
Business Utilities Only								
Miscellaneous								

Note #1:Home Office, Contractor payments, Depreciated Items and Self-Employed Health Insurance are summarized on dedicated pages a separate section of this book.

Note #2: Track your business miles and vehicle expenses in a separate mileage log to ensure accurate reporting and to determine the best deduction method for your situation.

Note #3: Cost of Goods is in another dedicated section of the book.

Note #4: I suggest you use a payroll program if you have employees that will require issuing a W2 for wages to ensure accurate reporting.

Date								
Vendor or Payee								
Description								Page Total
Advertising								
Commissions & Fees								
Employee Benefit Programs								
Insurance -Other								
Business Interest								
Legal & Professional Services								
Office Expenses								
Pension & Profit Sharing								
Rent or Lease								
Repairs & Maintenance								
Supplies								
Taxes & Licenses								
Travel								
Meals								
Business Utilities Only								
Miscellaneous								

Note #1:Home Office, Contractor payments, Depreciated Items and Self-Employed Health Insurance are summarized on dedicated pages a separate section of this book.

Note #2: Track your business miles and vehicle expenses in a separate mileage log to ensure accurate reporting and to determine the best deduction method for your situation.

Note #3: Cost of Goods is in another dedicated section of the book.

Note #4: I suggest you use a payroll program if you have employees that will require issuing a W2 for wages to ensure accurate reporting.

Date								
Vendor or Payee								
Description								Page Total
Advertising								
Commissions & Fees								
Employee Benefit Programs								
Insurance -Other								
Business Interest								
Legal & Professional Services								
Office Expenses								
Pension & Profit Sharing								
Rent or Lease								
Repairs & Maintenance								
Supplies								
Taxes & Licenses								
Travel								
Meals								
Business Utilities Only								
Miscellaneous								

Note #1:Home Office, Contractor payments, Depreciated Items and Self-Employed Health Insurance are summarized on dedicated pages a separate section of this book.

Note #2: Track your business miles and vehicle expenses in a separate mileage log to ensure accurate reporting and to determine the best deduction method for your situation.

Note #3: Cost of Goods is in another dedicated section of the book.

Note #4: I suggest you use a payroll program if you have employees that will require issuing a W2 for wages to ensure accurate reporting.

Date								
Vendor or Payee								
Description								Page Total
Advertising								
Commissions & Fees								
Employee Benefit Programs								
Insurance -Other								
Business Interest								
Legal & Professional Services								
Office Expenses								
Pension & Profit Sharing								
Rent or Lease								
Repairs & Maintenance								
Supplies								
Taxes & Licenses								
Travel								
Meals								
Business Utilities Only								
Miscellaneous								

Note #1:Home Office, Contractor payments, Depreciated Items and Self-Employed Health Insurance are summarized on dedicated pages a separate section of this book.

Note #2: Track your business miles and vehicle expenses in a separate mileage log to ensure accurate reporting and to determine the best deduction method for your situation.

Note #3: Cost of Goods is in another dedicated section of the book.

Note #4: I suggest you use a payroll program if you have employees that will require issuing a W2 for wages to ensure accurate reporting.

Date								
Vendor or Payee								
Description								Page Total
Advertising								
Commissions & Fees								
Employee Benefit Programs								
Insurance -Other								
Business Interest								
Legal & Professional Services								
Office Expenses								
Pension & Profit Sharing								
Rent or Lease								
Repairs & Maintenance								
Supplies								
Taxes & Licenses								
Travel								
Meals								
Business Utilities Only								
Miscellaneous								

Note #1:Home Office, Contractor payments, Depreciated Items and Self-Employed Health Insurance are summarized on dedicated pages a separate section of this book.

Note #2: Track your business miles and vehicle expenses in a separate mileage log to ensure accurate reporting and to determine the best deduction method for your situation.

Note #3: Cost of Goods is in another dedicated section of the book.

Note #4: I suggest you use a payroll program if you have employees that will require issuing a W2 for wages to ensure accurate reporting.

Date								
Vendor or Payee								
Description								Page Total
Advertising								
Commissions & Fees								
Employee Benefit Programs								
Insurance -Other								
Business Interest								
Legal & Professional Services								
Office Expenses								
Pension & Profit Sharing								
Rent or Lease								
Repairs & Maintenance								
Supplies								
Taxes & Licenses								
Travel								
Meals								
Business Utilities Only								
Miscellaneous								

Note #1:Home Office, Contractor payments, Depreciated Items and Self-Employed Health Insurance are summarized on dedicated pages a separate section of this book.

Note #2: Track your business miles and vehicle expenses in a separate mileage log to ensure accurate reporting and to determine the best deduction method for your situation.

Note #3: Cost of Goods is in another dedicated section of the book.

Note #4: I suggest you use a payroll program if you have employees that will require issuing a W2 for wages to ensure accurate reporting.

Date								
Vendor or Payee								
Description								Page Total
Advertising								
Commissions & Fees								
Employee Benefit Programs								
Insurance -Other								
Business Interest								
Legal & Professional Services								
Office Expenses								
Pension & Profit Sharing								
Rent or Lease								
Repairs & Maintenance								
Supplies								
Taxes & Licenses								
Travel								
Meals								
Business Utilities Only								
Miscellaneous								

Note #1:Home Office, Contractor payments, Depreciated Items and Self-Employed Health Insurance are summarized on dedicated pages a separate section of this book.

Note #2: Track your business miles and vehicle expenses in a separate mileage log to ensure accurate reporting and to determine the best deduction method for your situation.

Note #3: Cost of Goods is in another dedicated section of the book.

Note #4: I suggest you use a payroll program if you have employees that will require issuing a W2 for wages to ensure accurate reporting.

Date								
Vendor or Payee								
Description								Page Total
Advertising								
Commissions & Fees								
Employee Benefit Programs								
Insurance -Other								
Business Interest								
Legal & Professional Services								
Office Expenses								
Pension & Profit Sharing								
Rent or Lease								
Repairs & Maintenance								
Supplies								
Taxes & Licenses								
Travel								
Meals								
Business Utilities Only								
Miscellaneous								

Note #1:Home Office, Contractor payments, Depreciated Items and Self-Employed Health Insurance are summarized on dedicated pages a separate section of this book.

Note #2: Track your business miles and vehicle expenses in a separate mileage log to ensure accurate reporting and to determine the best deduction method for your situation.

Note #3: Cost of Goods is in another dedicated section of the book.

Note #4: I suggest you use a payroll program if you have employees that will require issuing a W2 for wages to ensure accurate reporting.

Date								
Vendor or Payee								
Description								Page Total
Advertising								
Commissions & Fees								
Employee Benefit Programs								
Insurance -Other								
Business Interest								
Legal & Professional Services								
Office Expenses								
Pension & Profit Sharing								
Rent or Lease								
Repairs & Maintenance								
Supplies								
Taxes & Licenses								
Travel								
Meals								
Business Utilities Only								
Miscellaneous								

Note #1:Home Office, Contractor payments, Depreciated Items and Self-Employed Health Insurance are summarized on dedicated pages a separate section of this book.

Note #2: Track your business miles and vehicle expenses in a separate mileage log to ensure accurate reporting and to determine the best deduction method for your situation.

Note #3: Cost of Goods is in another dedicated section of the book.

Note #4: I suggest you use a payroll program if you have employees that will require issuing a W2 for wages to ensure accurate reporting.

Date								
Vendor or Payee								
Description								Page Total
Advertising								
Commissions & Fees								
Employee Benefit Programs								
Insurance -Other								
Business Interest								
Legal & Professional Services								
Office Expenses								
Pension & Profit Sharing								
Rent or Lease								
Repairs & Maintenance								
Supplies								
Taxes & Licenses								
Travel								
Meals								
Business Utilities Only								
Miscellaneous								

Note #1:Home Office, Contractor payments, Depreciated Items and Self-Employed Health Insurance are summarized on dedicated pages a separate section of this book.

Note #2: Track your business miles and vehicle expenses in a separate mileage log to ensure accurate reporting and to determine the best deduction method for your situation.

Note #3: Cost of Goods is in another dedicated section of the book.

Note #4: I suggest you use a payroll program if you have employees that will require issuing a W2 for wages to ensure accurate reporting.

Date								
Vendor or Payee								
Description								Page Total
Advertising								
Commissions & Fees								
Employee Benefit Programs								
Insurance -Other								
Business Interest								
Legal & Professional Services								
Office Expenses								
Pension & Profit Sharing								
Rent or Lease								
Repairs & Maintenance								
Supplies								
Taxes & Licenses								
Travel								
Meals								
Business Utilities Only								
Miscellaneous								

Note #1:Home Office, Contractor payments, Depreciated Items and Self-Employed Health Insurance are summarized on dedicated pages a separate section of this book.

Note #2: Track your business miles and vehicle expenses in a separate mileage log to ensure accurate reporting and to determine the best deduction method for your situation.

Note #3: Cost of Goods is in another dedicated section of the book.

Note #4: I suggest you use a payroll program if you have employees that will require issuing a W2 for wages to ensure accurate reporting.

Date								
Vendor or Payee								
Description								Page Total
Advertising								
Commissions & Fees								
Employee Benefit Programs								
Insurance -Other								
Business Interest								
Legal & Professional Services								
Office Expenses								
Pension & Profit Sharing								
Rent or Lease								
Repairs & Maintenance								
Supplies								
Taxes & Licenses								
Travel								
Meals								
Business Utilities Only								
Miscellaneous								

Note #1:Home Office, Contractor payments, Depreciated Items and Self-Employed Health Insurance are summarized on dedicated pages a separate section of this book.

Note #2: Track your business miles and vehicle expenses in a separate mileage log to ensure accurate reporting and to determine the best deduction method for your situation.

Note #3: Cost of Goods is in another dedicated section of the book.

Note #4: I suggest you use a payroll program if you have employees that will require issuing a W2 for wages to ensure accurate reporting.

Date								
Vendor or Payee								
Description								Page Total
Advertising								
Commissions & Fees								
Employee Benefit Programs								
Insurance -Other								
Business Interest								
Legal & Professional Services								
Office Expenses								
Pension & Profit Sharing								
Rent or Lease								
Repairs & Maintenance								
Supplies								
Taxes & Licenses								
Travel								
Meals								
Business Utilities Only								
Miscellaneous								

Note #1:Home Office, Contractor payments, Depreciated Items and Self-Employed Health Insurance are summarized on dedicated pages a separate section of this book.

Note #2: Track your business miles and vehicle expenses in a separate mileage log to ensure accurate reporting and to determine the best deduction method for your situation.

Note #3: Cost of Goods is in another dedicated section of the book.

Note #4: I suggest you use a payroll program if you have employees that will require issuing a W2 for wages to ensure accurate reporting.

Date								
Vendor or Payee								
Description								Page Total
Advertising								
Commissions & Fees								
Employee Benefit Programs								
Insurance -Other								
Business Interest								
Legal & Professional Services								
Office Expenses								
Pension & Profit Sharing								
Rent or Lease								
Repairs & Maintenance								
Supplies								
Taxes & Licenses								
Travel								
Meals								
Business Utilities Only								
Miscellaneous								

Note #1:Home Office, Contractor payments, Depreciated Items and Self-Employed Health Insurance are summarized on dedicated pages a separate section of this book.

Note #2: Track your business miles and vehicle expenses in a separate mileage log to ensure accurate reporting and to determine the best deduction method for your situation.

Note #3: Cost of Goods is in another dedicated section of the book.

Note #4: I suggest you use a payroll program if you have employees that will require issuing a W2 for wages to ensure accurate reporting.

Date								
Vendor or Payee								
Description								Page Total
Advertising								
Commissions & Fees								
Employee Benefit Programs								
Insurance -Other								
Business Interest								
Legal & Professional Services								
Office Expenses								
Pension & Profit Sharing								
Rent or Lease								
Repairs & Maintenance								
Supplies								
Taxes & Licenses								
Travel								
Meals								
Business Utilities Only								
Miscellaneous								

Note #1:Home Office, Contractor payments, Depreciated Items and Self-Employed Health Insurance are summarized on dedicated pages a separate section of this book.

Note #2: Track your business miles and vehicle expenses in a separate mileage log to ensure accurate reporting and to determine the best deduction method for your situation.

Note #3: Cost of Goods is in another dedicated section of the book.

Note #4: I suggest you use a payroll program if you have employees that will require issuing a W2 for wages to ensure accurate reporting.

Date								
Vendor or Payee								
Description								Page Total
Advertising								
Commissions & Fees								
Employee Benefit Programs								
Insurance -Other								
Business Interest								
Legal & Professional Services								
Office Expenses								
Pension & Profit Sharing								
Rent or Lease								
Repairs & Maintenance								
Supplies								
Taxes & Licenses								
Travel								
Meals								
Business Utilities Only								
Miscellaneous								

Note #1:Home Office, Contractor payments, Depreciated Items and Self-Employed Health Insurance are summarized on dedicated pages a separate section of this book.

Note #2: Track your business miles and vehicle expenses in a separate mileage log to ensure accurate reporting and to determine the best deduction method for your situation.

Note #3: Cost of Goods is in another dedicated section of the book.

Note #4: I suggest you use a payroll program if you have employees that will require issuing a W2 for wages to ensure accurate reporting.

Date								
Vendor or Payee								
Description								Page Total
Advertising								
Commissions & Fees								
Employee Benefit Programs								
Insurance -Other								
Business Interest								
Legal & Professional Services								
Office Expenses								
Pension & Profit Sharing								
Rent or Lease								
Repairs & Maintenance								
Supplies								
Taxes & Licenses								
Travel								
Meals								
Business Utilities Only								
Miscellaneous								

Note #1:Home Office, Contractor payments, Depreciated Items and Self-Employed Health Insurance are summarized on dedicated pages a separate section of this book.

Note #2: Track your business miles and vehicle expenses in a separate mileage log to ensure accurate reporting and to determine the best deduction method for your situation.

Note #3: Cost of Goods is in another dedicated section of the book.

Note #4: I suggest you use a payroll program if you have employees that will require issuing a W2 for wages to ensure accurate reporting.

Date								
Vendor or Payee								
Description								Page Total
Advertising								
Commissions & Fees								
Employee Benefit Programs								
Insurance -Other								
Business Interest								
Legal & Professional Services								
Office Expenses								
Pension & Profit Sharing								
Rent or Lease								
Repairs & Maintenance								
Supplies								
Taxes & Licenses								
Travel								
Meals								
Business Utilities Only								
Miscellaneous								

Note #1:Home Office, Contractor payments, Depreciated Items and Self-Employed Health Insurance are summarized on dedicated pages a separate section of this book.

Note #2: Track your business miles and vehicle expenses in a separate mileage log to ensure accurate reporting and to determine the best deduction method for your situation.

Note #3: Cost of Goods is in another dedicated section of the book.

Note #4: I suggest you use a payroll program if you have employees that will require issuing a W2 for wages to ensure accurate reporting.

Date								
Vendor or Payee								
Description								Page Total
Advertising								
Commissions & Fees								
Employee Benefit Programs								
Insurance -Other								
Business Interest								
Legal & Professional Services								
Office Expenses								
Pension & Profit Sharing								
Rent or Lease								
Repairs & Maintenance								
Supplies								
Taxes & Licenses								
Travel								
Meals								
Business Utilities Only								
Miscellaneous								

Note #1:Home Office, Contractor payments, Depreciated Items and Self-Employed Health Insurance are summarized on dedicated pages a separate section of this book.

Note #2: Track your business miles and vehicle expenses in a separate mileage log to ensure accurate reporting and to determine the best deduction method for your situation.

Note #3: Cost of Goods is in another dedicated section of the book.

Note #4: I suggest you use a payroll program if you have employees that will require issuing a W2 for wages to ensure accurate reporting.

Date								
Vendor or Payee								
Description								Page Total
Advertising								
Commissions & Fees								
Employee Benefit Programs								
Insurance -Other								
Business Interest								
Legal & Professional Services								
Office Expenses								
Pension & Profit Sharing								
Rent or Lease								
Repairs & Maintenance								
Supplies								
Taxes & Licenses								
Travel								
Meals								
Business Utilities Only								
Miscellaneous								

Note #1:Home Office, Contractor payments, Depreciated Items and Self-Employed Health Insurance are summarized on dedicated pages a separate section of this book.

Note #2: Track your business miles and vehicle expenses in a separate mileage log to ensure accurate reporting and to determine the best deduction method for your situation.

Note #3: Cost of Goods is in another dedicated section of the book.

Note #4: I suggest you use a payroll program if you have employees that will require issuing a W2 for wages to ensure accurate reporting.

Date								
Vendor or Payee								
Description								Page Total
Advertising								
Commissions & Fees								
Employee Benefit Programs								
Insurance -Other								
Business Interest								
Legal & Professional Services								
Office Expenses								
Pension & Profit Sharing								
Rent or Lease								
Repairs & Maintenance								
Supplies								
Taxes & Licenses								
Travel								
Meals								
Business Utilities Only								
Miscellaneous								

Note #1:Home Office, Contractor payments, Depreciated Items and Self-Employed Health Insurance are summarized on dedicated pages a separate section of this book.

Note #2: Track your business miles and vehicle expenses in a separate mileage log to ensure accurate reporting and to determine the best deduction method for your situation.

Note #3: Cost of Goods is in another dedicated section of the book.

Note #4: I suggest you use a payroll program if you have employees that will require issuing a W2 for wages to ensure accurate reporting.

Date								
Vendor or Payee								
Description								Page Total
Advertising								
Commissions & Fees								
Employee Benefit Programs								
Insurance -Other								
Business Interest								
Legal & Professional Services								
Office Expenses								
Pension & Profit Sharing								
Rent or Lease								
Repairs & Maintenance								
Supplies								
Taxes & Licenses								
Travel								
Meals								
Business Utilities Only								
Miscellaneous								

Note #1:Home Office, Contractor payments, Depreciated Items and Self-Employed Health Insurance are summarized on dedicated pages a separate section of this book.

Note #2: Track your business miles and vehicle expenses in a separate mileage log to ensure accurate reporting and to determine the best deduction method for your situation.

Note #3: Cost of Goods is in another dedicated section of the book.

Note #4: I suggest you use a payroll program if you have employees that will require issuing a W2 for wages to ensure accurate reporting.

Date								
Vendor or Payee								
Description								Page Total
Advertising								
Commissions & Fees								
Employee Benefit Programs								
Insurance -Other								
Business Interest								
Legal & Professional Services								
Office Expenses								
Pension & Profit Sharing								
Rent or Lease								
Repairs & Maintenance								
Supplies								
Taxes & Licenses								
Travel								
Meals								
Business Utilities Only								
Miscellaneous								

Note #1:Home Office, Contractor payments, Depreciated Items and Self-Employed Health Insurance are summarized on dedicated pages a separate section of this book.

Note #2: Track your business miles and vehicle expenses in a separate mileage log to ensure accurate reporting and to determine the best deduction method for your situation.

Note #3: Cost of Goods is in another dedicated section of the book.

Note #4: I suggest you use a payroll program if you have employees that will require issuing a W2 for wages to ensure accurate reporting.

Date								
Vendor or Payee								
Description								Page Total
Advertising								
Commissions & Fees								
Employee Benefit Programs								
Insurance -Other								
Business Interest								
Legal & Professional Services								
Office Expenses								
Pension & Profit Sharing								
Rent or Lease								
Repairs & Maintenance								
Supplies								
Taxes & Licenses								
Travel								
Meals								
Business Utilities Only								
Miscellaneous								

Note #1:Home Office, Contractor payments, Depreciated Items and Self-Employed Health Insurance are summarized on dedicated pages a separate section of this book.

Note #2: Track your business miles and vehicle expenses in a separate mileage log to ensure accurate reporting and to determine the best deduction method for your situation.

Note #3: Cost of Goods is in another dedicated section of the book.

Note #4: I suggest you use a payroll program if you have employees that will require issuing a W2 for wages to ensure accurate reporting.

Date								
Vendor or Payee								
Description								Page Total
Advertising								
Commissions & Fees								
Employee Benefit Programs								
Insurance -Other								
Business Interest								
Legal & Professional Services								
Office Expenses								
Pension & Profit Sharing								
Rent or Lease								
Repairs & Maintenance								
Supplies								
Taxes & Licenses								
Travel								
Meals								
Business Utilities Only								
Miscellaneous								

Note #1:Home Office, Contractor payments, Depreciated Items and Self-Employed Health Insurance are summarized on dedicated pages a separate section of this book.

Note #2: Track your business miles and vehicle expenses in a separate mileage log to ensure accurate reporting and to determine the best deduction method for your situation.

Note #3: Cost of Goods is in another dedicated section of the book.

Note #4: I suggest you use a payroll program if you have employees that will require issuing a W2 for wages to ensure accurate reporting.

Date								
Vendor or Payee								
Description								Page Total
Advertising								
Commissions & Fees								
Employee Benefit Programs								
Insurance -Other								
Business Interest								
Legal & Professional Services								
Office Expenses								
Pension & Profit Sharing								
Rent or Lease								
Repairs & Maintenance								
Supplies								
Taxes & Licenses								
Travel								
Meals								
Business Utilities Only								
Miscellaneous								

Note #1:Home Office, Contractor payments, Depreciated Items and Self-Employed Health Insurance are summarized on dedicated pages a separate section of this book.

Note #2: Track your business miles and vehicle expenses in a separate mileage log to ensure accurate reporting and to determine the best deduction method for your situation.

Note #3: Cost of Goods is in another dedicated section of the book.

Note #4: I suggest you use a payroll program if you have employees that will require issuing a W2 for wages to ensure accurate reporting.

Date								
Vendor or Payee								
Description								Page Total
Advertising								
Commissions & Fees								
Employee Benefit Programs								
Insurance -Other								
Business Interest								
Legal & Professional Services								
Office Expenses								
Pension & Profit Sharing								
Rent or Lease								
Repairs & Maintenance								
Supplies								
Taxes & Licenses								
Travel								
Meals								
Business Utilities Only								
Miscellaneous								

Note #1:Home Office, Contractor payments, Depreciated Items and Self-Employed Health Insurance are summarized on dedicated pages a separate section of this book.

Note #2: Track your business miles and vehicle expenses in a separate mileage log to ensure accurate reporting and to determine the best deduction method for your situation.

Note #3: Cost of Goods is in another dedicated section of the book.

Note #4: I suggest you use a payroll program if you have employees that will require issuing a W2 for wages to ensure accurate reporting.

Date								
Vendor or Payee								
Description								Page Total
Advertising								
Commissions & Fees								
Employee Benefit Programs								
Insurance -Other								
Business Interest								
Legal & Professional Services								
Office Expenses								
Pension & Profit Sharing								
Rent or Lease								
Repairs & Maintenance								
Supplies								
Taxes & Licenses								
Travel								
Meals								
Business Utilities Only								
Miscellaneous								

Note #1:Home Office, Contractor payments, Depreciated Items and Self-Employed Health Insurance are summarized on dedicated pages a separate section of this book.

Note #2: Track your business miles and vehicle expenses in a separate mileage log to ensure accurate reporting and to determine the best deduction method for your situation.

Note #3: Cost of Goods is in another dedicated section of the book.

Note #4: I suggest you use a payroll program if you have employees that will require issuing a W2 for wages to ensure accurate reporting.

Date								
Vendor or Payee								
Description								Page Total
Advertising								
Commissions & Fees								
Employee Benefit Programs								
Insurance -Other								
Business Interest								
Legal & Professional Services								
Office Expenses								
Pension & Profit Sharing								
Rent or Lease								
Repairs & Maintenance								
Supplies								
Taxes & Licenses								
Travel								
Meals								
Business Utilities Only								
Miscellaneous								

Note #1:Home Office, Contractor payments, Depreciated Items and Self-Employed Health Insurance are summarized on dedicated pages a separate section of this book.

Note #2: Track your business miles and vehicle expenses in a separate mileage log to ensure accurate reporting and to determine the best deduction method for your situation.

Note #3: Cost of Goods is in another dedicated section of the book.

Note #4: I suggest you use a payroll program if you have employees that will require issuing a W2 for wages to ensure accurate reporting.

Date								
Vendor or Payee								
Description								Page Total
Advertising								
Commissions & Fees								
Employee Benefit Programs								
Insurance -Other								
Business Interest								
Legal & Professional Services								
Office Expenses								
Pension & Profit Sharing								
Rent or Lease								
Repairs & Maintenance								
Supplies								
Taxes & Licenses								
Travel								
Meals								
Business Utilities Only								
Miscellaneous								

Note #1:Home Office, Contractor payments, Depreciated Items and Self-Employed Health Insurance are summarized on dedicated pages a separate section of this book.

Note #2: Track your business miles and vehicle expenses in a separate mileage log to ensure accurate reporting and to determine the best deduction method for your situation.

Note #3: Cost of Goods is in another dedicated section of the book.

Note #4: I suggest you use a payroll program if you have employees that will require issuing a W2 for wages to ensure accurate reporting.

Date								
Vendor or Payee								
Description								Page Total
Advertising								
Commissions & Fees								
Employee Benefit Programs								
Insurance -Other								
Business Interest								
Legal & Professional Services								
Office Expenses								
Pension & Profit Sharing								
Rent or Lease								
Repairs & Maintenance								
Supplies								
Taxes & Licenses								
Travel								
Meals								
Business Utilities Only								
Miscellaneous								

Note #1:Home Office, Contractor payments, Depreciated Items and Self-Employed Health Insurance are summarized on dedicated pages a separate section of this book.

Note #2: Track your business miles and vehicle expenses in a separate mileage log to ensure accurate reporting and to determine the best deduction method for your situation.

Note #3: Cost of Goods is in another dedicated section of the book.

Note #4: I suggest you use a payroll program if you have employees that will require issuing a W2 for wages to ensure accurate reporting.

Date								
Vendor or Payee								
Description								Page Total
Advertising								
Commissions & Fees								
Employee Benefit Programs								
Insurance -Other								
Business Interest								
Legal & Professional Services								
Office Expenses								
Pension & Profit Sharing								
Rent or Lease								
Repairs & Maintenance								
Supplies								
Taxes & Licenses								
Travel								
Meals								
Business Utilities Only								
Miscellaneous								

Note #1:Home Office, Contractor payments, Depreciated Items and Self-Employed Health Insurance are summarized on dedicated pages a separate section of this book.

Note #2: Track your business miles and vehicle expenses in a separate mileage log to ensure accurate reporting and to determine the best deduction method for your situation.

Note #3: Cost of Goods is in another dedicated section of the book.

Note #4: I suggest you use a payroll program if you have employees that will require issuing a W2 for wages to ensure accurate reporting.

Annual Home Office Worksheets Section

Annual Home Office Worksheet for Office Space #1

Annual Home Office Worksheet for Office Space #2

Date office placed in service: ______________________

Date Office removed from service: ______________________

Office Square Footage: ______________________

Total Home Square Footage: ______________________

Home Office Type (Check One Reporting Method): ☐Regular ☐ Simplified

If used for daycare:

Days used per year: ________ Hours per day: __________

Expenses (Check whether Whole Property or Office Only):

Mortgage Interest: Whole Property ☐ Office Only ☐ Amount: ________

Real Estate Taxes: Whole property ☐ Office Only ☐ Amount: ________

Insurance: Whole property ☐ Office Only ☐ Amount: ________

Rent: Whole property ☐ Office Only ☐ Amount: ________

Repairs & Maintenance: Whole property ☐ Office Only ☐ Amount: ________

Utilities – Electric: Amount: ________

Utilities – Gas: Amount: ________

Utilities: Fuel Oil Amount:________

Utilities: Propane Amount:________

Utilities – Water: Amount: ________

Utilities – Trash: Amount: ________

Utilities – Alarm: Amount: ________

Utilities – Phone: Amount: ________

Utilities – Internet: Amount: ________

Utilities – Cable: Amount: ________

Other Costs:

HOA Fees: ______________________________

Condominium Fees: ______________________________

Landscaping/Mowing: ______________________________

Cleaning Services: ______________________________

Pest Control: ______________________________

Home's Adjusted Basis: ______________________________

Home's Fair Market Value: ______________________________

Land Value: ______________________________

Purchase Date: ______________________________

Date Placed in Service: ______________________________

Carryover Losses from Prior tax return year ________ form 8829 Line 43: ________

Carryover Losses from Prior tax return year ________form 8829 Line 44: ________

Annual Home Office Worksheet for Office Space #2

Date office placed in service: ______________________

Date Office removed from service: ______________________

Office Square Footage: ______________________

Total Home Square Footage: ______________________

Home Office Type (Check One Reporting Method): Regular ☐ Simplified ☐

If used for daycare:

Days used per year: ________ Hours per day: ________

Expenses (Check whether Whole Property or Office Only):

Mortgage Interest: Whole Property ☐ Office Only ☐ Amount: ________

Real Estate Taxes: Whole property ☐ Office Only ☐ Amount: ________

Insurance: Whole property ☐ Office Only ☐ Amount: ________

Rent: Whole property ☐ Office Only ☐ Amount: ________

Repairs & Maintenance: Whole property ☐ Office Only ☐ Amount: ________

Utilities – Electric: Amount: ________

Utilities – Gas: Amount: ________

Utilities: Fuel Oil Amount:________

Utilities: Propane Amount:________

Utilities – Water: Amount: ________

Utilities – Trash: Amount: ________

Utilities – Alarm: Amount: ________

Utilities – Phone: Amount: ________

Utilities – Internet: Amount: ________

Utilities – Cable: Amount: ________

Other Costs:

HOA Fees: ________________________________

Condominium Fees: ________________________________

Landscaping/Mowing: ________________________________

Cleaning Services: ________________________________

Pest Control: ________________________________

Home's Adjusted Basis: ________________________________

Home's Fair Market Value: ________________________________

Land Value: ________________________________

Purchase Date: ________________________________

Date Placed in Service: ________________________________

Carryover Losses from Prior tax return year ________ form 8829 Line 43: ________

Carryover Losses from Prior tax return year ________form 8829 Line 44: ________

Annual Home Office Worksheet for Office Space #3

Date office placed in service: ____________________

Date Office removed from service: ____________________

Office Square Footage: ____________________

Total Home Square Footage: ____________________

Home Office Type (Check One Reporting Method): Regular ☐ Simplified ☐

If used for daycare:

Days used per year: ________ Hours per day: ________

Expenses (Check whether Whole Property or Office Only):

Mortgage Interest: Whole Property ☐ Office Only ☐ Amount: ________

Real Estate Taxes: Whole property☐ Office Only ☐ Amount: ________

Insurance: Whole property ☐ Office Only ☐ Amount: ________

Rent: Whole property ☐ Office Only ☐ Amount: ________

Repairs & Maintenance: Whole property ☐ Office Only ☐ Amount: ________

Utilities – Electric: Amount: ________

Utilities – Gas: Amount: ________

Utilities: Fuel Oil Amount:________

Utilities: Propane Amount:________

Utilities – Water: Amount: ________

Utilities – Trash: Amount: ________

Utilities – Alarm: Amount: ________

Utilities – Phone: Amount: ________

Utilities – Internet: Amount: ________

Utilities – Cable: Amount: ________

Other Costs:

HOA Fees: ______________________________

Condominium Fees: ______________________________

Landscaping/Mowing: ______________________________

Cleaning Services: ______________________________

Pest Control: ______________________________

Home's Adjusted Basis: ______________________________

Home's Fair Market Value: ______________________________

Land Value: ______________________________

Purchase Date: ______________________________

Date Placed in Service: ______________________________

Carryover Losses from Prior tax return year ________ form 8829 Line 43: ________

Carryover Losses from Prior tax return year ________form 8829 Line 44: ________

Annual Home Office Worksheet for Office Space #4

Date office placed in service: ____________________

Date Office removed from service: ____________________

Office Square Footage: ____________________

Total Home Square Footage: ____________________

Home Office Type (Check One Reporting Method): Regular ☐ Simplified ☐

If used for daycare:

Days used per year: ________ Hours per day: ________

Expenses (Check whether Whole Property or Office Only):

Mortgage Interest: Whole Property ☐ Office Only ☐ Amount: ________

Real Estate Taxes: Whole property ☐ Office Only ☐ Amount: ________

Insurance: Whole property ☐ Office Only ☐ Amount: ________

Rent: Whole property ☐ Office Only ☐ Amount: ________

Repairs & Maintenance: Whole property ☐ Office Only ☐ Amount: ________

Utilities – Electric: Amount: ________

Utilities – Gas: Amount: ________

Utilities: Fuel Oil Amount:________

Utilities: Propane Amount:________

Utilities – Water: Amount: ________

Utilities – Trash: Amount: ________

Utilities – Alarm: Amount: ________

Utilities – Phone: Amount: ________

Utilities – Internet: Amount: ________

Utilities – Cable: Amount: ________

Other Costs:

HOA Fees: ______________________________

Condominium Fees: ______________________________

Landscaping/Mowing: ______________________________

Cleaning Services: ______________________________

Pest Control: ______________________________

Home's Adjusted Basis: ______________________________

Home's Fair Market Value: ______________________________

Land Value: ______________________________

Purchase Date: ______________________________

Date Placed in Service: ______________________________

Carryover Losses from Prior tax return year ________ form 8829 Line 43: ________

Carryover Losses from Prior tax return year ________form 8829 Line 44: ________

Annual Self-Employed Health Insurance Worksheet

Ineligible Premiums:

- Employer-sponsored group plan coverage
- Amounts paid with pre-tax dollars

Medical Insurance Premiums: ____________________

Dental Insurance Premiums: ____________________

Vision Insurance Premiums: ____________________

Medicare Part B Premiums: ____________________

Medicare Part D Premiums: ____________________

Medigap Premiums: ____________________

Supplemental coverage: ____________________

Long-Term Care Premiums Spouse name ____________________(Limits apply):$__________

Long-Term Care Premiums Spouse name ____________________(Limits apply):$__________

Cancer/Specified Disease Premiums: ____________________

Air Ambulance Coverage Premiums: ____________________

Notes:

Contract Labor Records For Preparing 1099s

W-9 vs. W-8BEN & When 1099s Are Required

When you hire someone to perform work for your business and they are *not* your employee, you should collect a Form W-9 from U.S. persons (including U.S. citizens, resident aliens, and U.S. entities) so you have their correct name, address, and Taxpayer Identification Number (TIN) for your records. This information is needed to prepare a 1099 if required.

A Form W-8BEN (or other W-8 series form) is used instead when the worker or contractor is a foreign person or entity with respect to U.S. tax law — it certifies foreign status and helps you apply the correct withholding rules.

For tax year 2025, you generally must issue a Form 1099-NEC or 1099-MISC to each non-employee contractor or vendor you paid $600 or more during the year in the course of your trade or business. These forms are filed with the IRS and furnished to the payee early in the following year.

Starting with tax year 2026 and beyond, reporting thresholds for Forms 1099-NEC and 1099-MISC will increase — e.g., payments totaling $2,000 or more in a year will generally be the new threshold for issuing these forms, reducing the number of small-amount 1099s you need to file.

Future thresholds will also be indexed for inflation.

W-2 Wage section is not included:

W-2 wages are not tracked in this workbook.

For proper compliance, use a payroll service or payroll software for employee wages and filings.

Contractor #1

Name:____

Address:____

Address:____

Address:____

Form on file: W-9 (U.S.) or W-8BEN (Foreign) *(circle one)*

Date paid____________________ Amount $_________________

Date paid____________________ Amount $_________________

Date paid____________________ Amount $_________________

Date paid____________________ Amount $_________________

Date paid____________________ Amount $_________________

Date paid____________________ Amount $_________________

Date paid____________________ Amount $_________________

Date paid____________________ Amount $_________________

Date paid____________________ Amount $_________________

Date paid____________________ Amount $_________________

Date paid____________________ Amount $_________________

Date paid____________________ Amount $_________________

Date paid____________________ Amount $_________________

Date paid____________________ Amount $_________________

Date paid____________________ Amount $_________________

Date paid____________________ Amount $_________________

Date paid____________________ Amount $_________________

Date paid____________________ Amount $_________________

Date paid____________________ Amount $_________________

Total $_________________

Contractor #2

Name:____

Address:____

Address:____

Address:____

Form on file: W-9 (U.S.) or W-8BEN (Foreign) *(circle one)*

Date paid____________________ Amount $_________________

Date paid____________________ Amount $_________________

Date paid____________________ Amount $_________________

Date paid____________________ Amount $_________________

Date paid____________________ Amount $_________________

Date paid____________________ Amount $_________________

Date paid____________________ Amount $_________________

Date paid____________________ Amount $_________________

Date paid____________________ Amount $_________________

Date paid____________________ Amount $_________________

Date paid____________________ Amount $_________________

Date paid____________________ Amount $_________________

Date paid____________________ Amount $_________________

Date paid____________________ Amount $_________________

Date paid____________________ Amount $_________________

Date paid____________________ Amount $_________________

Date paid____________________ Amount $_________________

Date paid____________________ Amount $_________________

Date paid____________________ Amount $_________________

Total $_________________

Contractor #3

Name:____

Address:____

Address:____

Address:____

Form on file: W-9 (U.S.) or W-8BEN (Foreign) *(circle one)*

Date paid____________________ Amount $__________________

Date paid____________________ Amount $__________________

Date paid____________________ Amount $__________________

Date paid____________________ Amount $__________________

Date paid____________________ Amount $__________________

Date paid____________________ Amount $__________________

Date paid____________________ Amount $__________________

Date paid____________________ Amount $__________________

Date paid____________________ Amount $__________________

Date paid____________________ Amount $__________________

Date paid____________________ Amount $__________________

Date paid____________________ Amount $__________________

Date paid____________________ Amount $__________________

Date paid____________________ Amount $__________________

Date paid____________________ Amount $__________________

Date paid____________________ Amount $__________________

Date paid____________________ Amount $__________________

Date paid____________________ Amount $__________________

Date paid____________________ Amount $__________________

Total $__________________

Contractor #4

Name:____

Address:____

Address:____

Address:____

Form on file: W-9 (U.S.) or W-8BEN (Foreign) *(circle one)*

Date paid______________________ Amount $___________________

Date paid______________________ Amount $___________________

Date paid______________________ Amount $___________________

Date paid______________________ Amount $___________________

Date paid______________________ Amount $___________________

Date paid______________________ Amount $___________________

Date paid______________________ Amount $___________________

Date paid______________________ Amount $___________________

Date paid______________________ Amount $___________________

Date paid______________________ Amount $___________________

Date paid______________________ Amount $___________________

Date paid______________________ Amount $___________________

Date paid______________________ Amount $___________________

Date paid______________________ Amount $___________________

Date paid______________________ Amount $___________________

Date paid______________________ Amount $___________________

Date paid______________________ Amount $___________________

Date paid______________________ Amount $___________________

Date paid______________________ Amount $___________________

Total $___________________

Contractor #5

Name:____

Address:______________________________________

Address:______________________________________

Address:______________________________________

Form on file: W-9 (U.S.) or W-8BEN (Foreign) *(circle one)*

Date paid__________________ Amount $________________

Date paid__________________ Amount $________________

Date paid__________________ Amount $________________

Date paid__________________ Amount $________________

Date paid__________________ Amount $________________

Date paid__________________ Amount $________________

Date paid__________________ Amount $________________

Date paid__________________ Amount $________________

Date paid__________________ Amount $________________

Date paid__________________ Amount $________________

Date paid__________________ Amount $________________

Date paid__________________ Amount $________________

Date paid__________________ Amount $________________

Date paid__________________ Amount $________________

Date paid__________________ Amount $________________

Date paid__________________ Amount $________________

Date paid__________________ Amount $________________

Date paid__________________ Amount $________________

Date paid__________________ Amount $________________

Total $________________

Depreciation list of Items

Item	Date of Purchase	Date placed in Service	Cost	% of business use

Item	Date of Purchase	Date placed in Service	Cost	% of business use

Cost of Goods Sold (COGS)

Important: Cost of Goods Sold (COGS) rules are technical and must be applied correctly to avoid overstating deductions or misstating income.

How costs are classified, timed, and matched to revenue matters.

This section is intentionally brief. If you are unsure how to use this section in coordination with expenses recorded elsewhere in this book, consult a qualified tax professional to ensure proper treatment and compliance.

Method used to value closing inventory (circle one):

Cost   Lower of Cost or Market   Other (explain): __________

Inventory at the beginning of the year $__________________

Purchases $__________________

Items Withdrawn for personal use $__________________

Cost of Labor. Do not include amount
Paid to yourself $__________________

Materials and supplies $__________________

Other costs $__________________

Inventory at the end of the year $__________________

For Your Tax Professional:

This workbook is designed to support accurate, well-organized recordkeeping for Schedule C filers.

Expenses, worksheets, and summaries are grouped by common IRS reporting categories and maintained separately where required for clarity (such as home office, mileage, self-employed health insurance, depreciation, and cost of goods sold).

When used consistently throughout the year, this format is intended to reduce reclassification, follow-up questions, and year-end reconstruction, allowing your tax professional to focus on proper application of the tax law rather than recreating records.

Year-End Checklist

✓ Reconcile bank and credit card statements

✓ Ensure all receipts are categorized and retained

✓ Verify Home Office Worksheet is completed

✓ Verify Annual Self-Employed Health Insurance worksheet has been completed

✓ Update mileage totals in your Mileage Log Book

✓ Compile contract labor records

✓ Issue 1099 forms by **January 31** of the following year, if required

✓ Compile depreciable items

✓ Generate W-2 forms by **January 31** of the following year, if required

✓ Compile cost of goods if needed

✓ Calculate and fund any Employer matching retirement account contributions

✓ Calculate and fund any Employee retirement account contributions

✓ Confirm all totals are accurate

✓ Review expenses for potential missing deductions

✓ Prepare documents for tax filing

Notes

Notes: ____________________________________

Additional Notes: ________________________________

Additional Notes: ______________________________

Printed in Dunstable, United Kingdom

91223997R00071